Pennsylvania

by the Capstone Press
Geography Department

CAPSTONE PRESS
MANKATO, MINNESOTA

CAPSTONE PRESS

818 North Willow Street • Mankato, MN 56001

Printed in the United States of America.

Library of Congress Cataloging-in-Publication Data
    Pennsylvania/by the Capstone Press Geography Department
    p. cm.--(One Nation)
    Includes bibliographical references and index.
    Summary: Gives an overview of the state of Pennsylvania, including its
history, geography, people, and living conditions.
    ISBN 1-56065-438-4
    1. Pennsylvania--Juvenile literature. [1. Pennsylvania.]
    I. Capstone Press. Geography Dept. II. Series.
F149.3.P46 1996
974.8--dc20

                                                        96-23442
                                                           CIP
                                                            AC

Photo credits
G. Alan Nelson, cover, 10, 15, 30.
Flag Research Center, 4 (left).
Tom Stack and Associates, 4 (right), 5
James Rowan, 6, 25, 26, 28, 32, 34.
Root Resources, 8, 22, 44.
Lynn Seldon, 16, 18, 21.

Table of Contents

Fast Facts about Pennsylvania 4

Chapter 1 The Liberty Bell 7

Chapter 2 The Land 11

Chapter 3 The People 17

Chapter 4 Pennsylvania History 23

Chapter 5 Pennsylvania Business 31

Chapter 6 Seeing the Sights 35

Pennsylvania Time Line 40

Famous Pennsylvanians.................................. 42

Glossary 45

To Learn More 46

Internet Sites 46

Useful Addresses 47

Index 48

Words in **boldface** type in the text are defined in the Glossary in the back of this book.

Fast Facts about Pennsylvania

State Flag

Location: In the Middle Atlantic region of the northeastern United States.
Size: 46,058 square miles (119,751 square kilometers)

Population: 11,881,643 (1990 United States Census Bureau figures)
Capital: Harrisburg
Date admitted to the Union: December 12, 1787; the second state

Ruffed grouse

Mountain laurel

Largest cities:
Philadelphia,
Pittsburgh, Erie,
Allentown,
Scranton,
Reading,
Bethlehem,
Lancaster,
Harrisburg,
Altoona

Nickname: The
Keystone State
State animal:
White-tailed
deer
State bird: Ruffed
grouse
State flower:
Mountain laurel
State tree:
Hemlock
State song: None

Hemlock

5

Chapter 1
The Liberty Bell

Philadelphia, Pennsylvania, has one of the world's best-known bells. This bell no longer rings. Thousands of people come to see it every day, however. It is the Liberty Bell.

The bell was made in England. It was for the Pennsylvania **colony's** State House. Philadelphians hung it in the bell tower in 1753. They rang the bell on special occasions.

Ringing for Independence

Pennsylvania's State House was renamed Independence Hall. On July 4, 1776, colonial leaders met there. They declared the colonies independent from England.

Colonial leaders met at Independence Hall in Philadelphia. On July 4, 1776, they declared their independence.

Visitors can see the Liberty Bell's famous crack.

On July 8, the Declaration of Independence was read in public. The bell was rung in celebration. The United States of America had begun.

The Crack in the Liberty Bell

Every year until 1835, the bell sounded on July 4. On July 8, 1835, the bell rang for a funeral. Suddenly, the bell cracked.

From 1835 to 1976, the Liberty Bell stood quietly. It was then moved to the nearby Liberty Bell Pavilion. This building stands in Independence National Historic Park. Visitors can see the bell and its famous crack. The park and the bell honor America's liberty.

The Keystone State

Pennsylvania's nickname is the Keystone State. It got its nickname because it stood in the middle of the 13 original states.

Pennsylvania gave strength to the new United States. The United States Constitution was written in Independence Hall. Philadelphia served as the nation's capital from 1790 to 1800.

Pittsburgh was called the Gateway to the West. From there, pioneers headed to the western frontier. Later, the state's coal and oil heated American homes.

Pennsylvania is still important to the nation. It is a leading manufacturing and shipping state. Pittsburgh glass and paints are used throughout the nation. The world's largest chocolate factory is in Hershey.

Chapter 2
The Land

Pennsylvania is in the northeastern United States. It is known as a mid-Atlantic state. This state is not on the Atlantic Ocean, however.

The three other mid-Atlantic states border Pennsylvania. They are New York, New Jersey, and Delaware. These states are on the Atlantic Ocean.

Mountains cover much of Pennsylvania. Lowlands are in the northwest and southeast corners. The state also has river valleys, rolling hills, and forests.

A mill stands on Slippery Rock Creek. The state has mountains, river valleys, rolling hills, and forests.

Lake Erie

Ohio

New Jersey

Allegheny River

Allegheny Plateau

Susquehanna River

Delaware River

Appalachian Mountains

Philadephia

Allegheny Mountains

Blue Ridge Mountains

Schuylkill River

Ohio River

Juniata River

Harrisburg

Delaware

Pittsburgh

Mt. Davis

Maryland

West Virginia

Pennsylvania's Lowlands

The Erie Lowland is in northwestern Pennsylvania. It borders Lake Erie. The land there is rich. Potatoes and grapes grow well there.

The Atlantic Coastal Plain crosses Pennsylvania's southeastern corner. The state's lowest point is there. This is sea level along the Delaware River. The Schuykill River empties into

12

the Delaware River. Philadelphia sits between the two rivers.

The Appalachian Mountains

The Appalachian Mountain Range covers most of the rest of Pennsylvania. The Allegheny Mountains are part of this range. So are the Pocono and Blue Ridge mountains.

Mount Davis is in the southern Alleghenies. It reaches 3,213 feet (964 meters) above sea level. This is Pennsylvania's highest point.

The Pocono Mountains are in northeastern Pennsylvania. Waterfalls tumble over cliffs in the Poconos. More than 200 lakes lie within these mountains. Lake Wallenpaupack is the largest one.

The Blue Ridge Mountains rise in the southeast. Hemlock, oak, and pine trees grow on their slopes. These mountains continue into Maryland.

Narrow river valleys cut through the Alleghenies. The Susquehanna River winds through the northeast.

In the west, the Allegheny River winds south. The Monongahela River flows north. These rivers meet in Pittsburgh. They form the Ohio River. The river then flows west into the state of Ohio.

The Piedmont

Southeast of the mountains lies the **Piedmont**. Low hills roll over the land there. This is some of the nation's richest farmland. Corn, peaches, and apples grow well there.

Climate

Pennsylvania has warm summers and cold winters. Eastern Pennsylvania is generally warmer and wetter than western Pennsylvania.

Northwestern Pennsylvania receives the most snow. About 90 inches (229 centimeters) fall there each winter. Strong blizzards cross the shores of Lake Erie.

In the spring, rain and melting snow sometimes cause floods. The Johnstown flood in 1889 killed 2,200 people. A flood there in 1977 claimed 68 lives.

The Allegheny River valley is in western Pennsylvania.

Plants and Animals

Forests cover three-fifths of the state. Pennsylvania has more wilderness than any other eastern state. White-tailed deer, black bear, and raccoons live in the forests.

The state bird is the ruffed grouse. Quail, pheasants, and geese also live in Pennsylvania. Bass, trout, and perch swim in its lakes and rivers.

Chapter 3

The People

By population, Pennsylvania is the fifth-largest state. It also has the nation's fifth-largest city. This is Philadelphia.

Almost 70 percent of Pennsylvanians live in or near cities. Land around Philadelphia, Pittsburgh, and Erie is the most crowded.

Nearly 4 million people live on farms or in small towns. No other state has that many **rural** people.

European Immigrants

Almost 89 percent of Pennsylvanians are white. Many of them are **descendants** of early European settlers.

People can visit colonial houses in Philadelphia.

The Amish drive horse-drawn buggies.

Pennsylvania's first colonists arrived in the 1600s. They came from Holland, Finland, and Sweden. German, French, English, Welsh, and Scotch-Irish people soon joined them.

Many Irish **immigrants** arrived in the 1840s. In the 1880s, more Europeans came to Pennsylvania. They arrived from Italy, Czechoslovakia, Poland, and Russia. These immigrants worked in Pennsylvania's mills, mines, and factories.

The Pennsylvania Dutch

German-speaking farmers settled throughout southeastern Pennsylvania. Today, these people are known as the Pennsylvania Dutch. The word Dutch comes from *Deutsch*, which is the German word for "German." German towns still dot the Schuykill valley.

Many Pennsylvania Dutch people live in Lancaster County. They are Amish. They believe in living simply. Their farmhouses have no electricity or telephones. They drive to town in horse-drawn buggies.

African Americans

African Americans have lived in Pennsylvania since the 1680s. Many were slaves. Some, however, were free. They owned shops or worked at trades.

In 1780, Pennsylvania passed an antislavery law. It said that all African Americans born in Pennsylvania were free. In 1820, Philadelphia opened the nation's first public school for African Americans.

Pennsylvania had many stops on the Underground Railroad. This was a system of hiding places for southern slaves. They were escaping to freedom in Canada. Slavery was legal in the South until 1865.

In the 1900s, more African Americans left the South. Many of them moved to Pennsylvania. Today, more than 9 percent of Pennsylvanians are African American. Philadelphia has many African-American neighborhoods.

Hispanic Americans

Two percent of Pennsylvanians are Hispanic. Puerto Ricans make up more than 143,000 of these Spanish-speaking people. Many Hispanic Americans also came from Mexico and Cuba. They have neighborhoods in Philadelphia and other cities.

Asian Americans

Almost 140,000 Asian Americans live in Pennsylvania. Many of them came from India, China, Japan, and the Philippines. Recently, people have arrived from Korea, Laos, Thailand, and Vietnam.

South Philadelphia has a large Italian outdoor market.

Native Americans

More than 14,000 Native Americans live in Pennsylvania. Most of their **ancestors** were Algonquin. They once lived in Appalachian forests or along the coast.

Today's Native Americans live throughout the state. There are no **reservations** in Pennsylvania.

Chapter 4
Pennsylvania History

People lived in Pennsylvania about 12,000 years ago. Four Native American groups lived there by the 1600s. They were the Delaware, Susquehannock, Monongahela, and Erie Indians. They lived along bodies of water that are now named after them.

European Explorers and Settlers

Dutch explorers reached Pennsylvania in 1614. In 1638, Swedish settlers founded New Sweden. They built Pennsylvania's first non-Indian town. It was Fort New Gothenburg on Tinicum Island.

A Dutch fleet captured New Sweden in 1655. Nine years later, the English drove out the Dutch.

The Pennsylvania Monument stands at Gettysburg. It is the site of the biggest battle of the Civil War.

William Penn's Colony

In 1681, England's king granted Pennsylvania to William Penn. The colony's name meant "Penn's Woods."

Penn belonged to the Quaker religion. He welcomed Catholics and Jews to the colony. Lutherans, Baptists, and Amish came also.

In 1682, Penn founded the city of Philadelphia. He also signed treaties with nearby Native Americans.

French and English Conflict

By 1732, England had 13 colonies along the Atlantic. The French were also settling North America. They built forts in western Pennsylvania. This caused a war between England and France.

By 1763, the English controlled all of Pennsylvania. They built Fort Pitt. Pittsburgh stands there today.

The Revolutionary War

To pay for the war, England raised taxes. The colonists refused to pay the taxes.

George Washington's headquarters still stands at Valley Forge. His troops spent a harsh winter there.

Starting in 1774, leaders from each colony met in Philadelphia. In 1775, they appointed George Washington head of the army. On July 4, 1776, they approved the Declaration of Independence.

In September 1777, English armies invaded Pennsylvania. Washington's army lost the battles of Brandywine Creek and Germantown.

The English occupied Philadelphia in October. Washington's troops spent a harsh winter at nearby Valley Forge. In 1778, the English left Philadelphia.

England **surrendered** in 1781. A peace treaty was signed in 1783.

A New Nation, a New State

The Constitutional Convention met in Philadelphia in 1787. Its leaders wrote the United States Constitution. Pennsylvania **ratified** the Constitution on December 12, 1787. It became the second state. Philadelphia served as the new nation's capital from 1790 to 1800.

Pennsylvania became a center of trade. In 1812, steamboats began chugging down the Ohio River. Canals, roads, and railroads carried goods throughout the state.

Mining of coal and iron ore grew in the west. In 1859, the nation's first oil well gushed at Titusville.

The Civil War

By 1860, the issue of slavery divided the nation. In 1861, the Civil War began. Pennsylvania sent 340,000 troops to fight for the Union of the North.

A statue of George Washington stands by Independence Hall.

The Battle of Gettysburg was fought in July 1863.

In July 1863, America's biggest battle took place. The Battle of Gettysburg was an important Union victory. The southern armies retreated. The Confederacy surrendered in 1865.

The Steel Industry

In 1873, Pittsburgh had the nation's first steel mill. Steel went into new skyscrapers, ships, and bridges. Pennsylvania coal powered blast furnaces in the mills.

During World War I (1914-1918), Pennsylvania made ships, weapons, and steel. These goods helped the United States win the war.

The Great Depression (1929-1939) brought hard times to the nation. Mines and steel mills closed. Unemployment reached 80 percent among Pennsylvania's miners and steelworkers.

World War II (1939-1945) helped end the Depression. Pennsylvania steel went into tanks, ships, and weapons.

Recent Problems and Changes

After the war, other states and countries produced more steel. The nation's need for coal decreased. Many Pennsylvania workers lost their jobs.

Pennsylvania also struggled with pollution. It is working to clean up its rivers and Lake Erie.

To gain more jobs, the state has attracted new industries. Thousands of Pennsylvanians now work for computer companies.

More jobs are also available in the tourism industry. Philadelphia and Pittsburgh have developed their historic sites. Hotels and ski resorts have boomed in the mountains.

Chapter 5

Pennsylvania Business

Service industries play the biggest part in Pennsylvania's economy. About 4 million Pennsylvanians have service jobs. Banks, insurance companies, and stores are some service businesses.

Manufacturing, farming, and mining are still important in Pennsylvania. About 940,000 Pennsylvanians make products. Farm workers total more than 100,000. Almost 22,000 Pennsylvanians are miners.

Service Industries

Philadelphia, Pittsburgh, and Reading have many large banks. Philadelphia is famous for its law firms.

Corn and wheat grow on a Lancaster Country farm.

Philadephia is one of the nation's busiest ports.

Pittsburgh's and Philadelphia's ports are among the nation's busiest. Coal and oil are shipped from these ports.

Tourism has become an important service industry. Visitors spend more than $10 billion in Pennsylvania each year. Restaurants, hotels, and resorts receive much of this money.

Manufacturing

Food products and chemicals lead Pennsylvania's manufactured goods. Pennsylvania leads the nation in canning mushrooms. Chocolate, ice cream, and potato chips are other leading foods. Medicines and paint top the chemical list.

Pennsylvania is third among the states at making steel. Computers and machine tools are other important products.

Agriculture

Eastern Pennsylvania's dairy farms produce much milk. This is the state's leading farm product.

Mushrooms are the state's leading crop. Piedmont farmers grow corn, hay, oats, potatoes, and tobacco. Grapes grow near Lake Erie. Apples and peaches grow in southern Pennsylvania.

Tree farms raise spruces and pines for Christmas trees. Some farmers tap maple trees. They make maple syrup.

Mining

Eastern Pennsylvania produces the nation's only anthracite coal. Western Pennsylvania provides large amounts of bituminous coal. Anthracite is hard coal and bituminous is soft coal.

Limestone is another Pennsylvania mineral. Most of it comes from the Piedmont.

Western Pennsylvania has large deposits of natural gas. A few wells still produce oil.

Chapter 6
Seeing the Sights

Travelers have much to see and do in Pennsylvania. Philadelphia and other cities offer historic sites. Many visitors enjoy the state's mountains, forests, and lakes.

Philadelphia

Philadelphia is Pennsylvania's largest city. City Hall stands in the center of the city. Atop the building is a statue of William Penn. The statue is 37 feet (11 meters) tall.

To the east is Independence Hall. The nation's founders signed the Declaration of Independence there.

Philadelphia is also the site of a United States mint. About 1.5 million coins are made there every hour.

Presque Isle State Park on Lake Erie attracts many visitors.

South Philadelphia has a large Italian outdoor market. Shoppers buy flowers, fresh fish, and clothing. Hungry Philadelphians eat Philly cheesesteak sandwiches there.

Northwest of Philadelphia

Valley Forge lies northwest of Philadelphia. George Washington's troops spent the winter of 1777-1778 there. Washington's headquarters still stands on the site. The troops' huts have been rebuilt.

Farther northwest is the Hopewell Furnace. This is a restored blast furnace. It made iron goods from 1771 to 1883.

Northeastern Pennsylvania

Bethlehem is north of Philadelphia. It is a famous steel city. An 18th century industrial neighborhood has been restored there. Visitors can see a mill, a tannery, and a waterworks.

To the northeast is the Delaware Water Gap. The Delaware River cut a path through the Kittatinny Mountains. Hikers can walk to Dingmans Falls and Silver Thread Falls.

To the west stand the Pocono Mountains. Parks, resorts, and campgrounds are found throughout the mountains. Skiers and snowmobilers enjoy the Poconos in the winter. Summer visitors hike, swim, and go boating.

Scranton is to the north. Coal mining and steelmaking once boomed in this town. Today, visitors can tour the Lackawanna Coal Mine. It is 300 feet (90 meters) underground.

Central Pennsylvania

Williamsport is southwest of Scranton. It is the birthplace of Little League baseball. Each year, the town hosts the Little League World Series.

To the south is Harrisburg. This is the state capital. The capitol building has 651 rooms. Its dome is 272 feet (82 meters) high.

Near Harrisburg is the Three Mile Island nuclear power plant. A dangerous accident occured there in 1979.

York is farther south. Taverns, homes, and churches from colonial days still stand there.

York is also home to a Harley-Davidson assembly plant. The plant is open for guided tours.

To the southwest is Gettysburg National Military Park. It preserves the Gettysburg Battlefield. Hundreds of Civil War cannons stand on the hills. More than 1,300 monuments mark where different units fought.

Western Pennsylvania

The steep Alleghenies surround the city of Altoona. The city was once a major railroad center. Today, visitors enjoy the Railroaders Memorial Museum. A collection of locomotives is on display there.

To the northwest is Punxsutawney. A famous groundhog lives there. On Groundhog Day on February 2, Punxsutawney Phil comes out of his hole. It is said that if this groundhog sees his shadow, winter will last six more weeks.

Pittsburgh

Pittsburgh lies in southwestern Pennsylvania. The Fort Pitt Museum is there. Visitors learn about the French and English struggle for Pennsylvania.

The Carnegie was built by Andrew Carnegie. He also built Pittsburgh's first steel mill. The Carnegie includes a library, a music hall, and two museums.

Steep hills surround Pittsburgh. Trolleys climb the slopes for a view of the city. Passengers ride them up and down Mount Washington. From the top, they can look down on Pittsburgh.

Pennsylvania Time Line

10,000 B.C.—The first people arrive in Pennsylvania.

1615—Cornelius Hendrickson, a Dutch explorer, sails up the Delaware River to present-day Philadelphia.

1638—The colony of New Sweden is founded along the Delaware River.

1682—William Penn founds the Pennsylvania Colony.

1731—Benjamin Franklin begins the first library in the colonies.

1776—The Declaration of Independence is adopted in Philadelphia.

1787—Pennsylvania becomes the second state.

1812—Harrisburg becomes the permanent capital of Pennsylvania.

1829—The first commercial railroad begins running in Pennsylvania.

1857—Pennsylvanian James Buchanan becomes the 15th president of the United States.

1859—Oil is discovered near Titusville.

1863—The Battle of Gettysburg is fought.

1873—Andrew Carnegie opens the nation's first steel mill in Pittsburgh.

1889—The Johnstown Flood kills 2,200 people.

1920—Station KDKA in Pittsburgh makes the first public radio broadcast in the nation.

1956—The Pennsylvania Turnpike is completed.

1957—The nation's first nuclear power plant opens in Shippingport.

1979—A serious accident occurs at the Three Mile Island nuclear plant near Harrisburg.

1984—W. Wilson Goode becomes Philadelphia's first African-American mayor.

1988—About 1 million gallons of oil spill into the Monongahela and Ohio rivers near Pittsburgh.

Famous Pennsylvanians

Guion Bluford Jr. (1942-) First African-American astronaut; flew aboard the space shuttle Challenger; born in Philadelphia.

Daniel Boone (1734-1820) Frontiersman who guided pioneers into Kentucky; born near present-day Reading.

Rachel Carson (1907-1964) Marine biologist and author; wrote *Silent Spring* about dangers to the environment; born in Springdale.

Mary Cassatt (1847-1926) Artist who specialized in mother and child paintings; born in Allegheny City.

Wilt Chamberlain (1936-) Professional basketball player who scored 100 points in a game in 1962; born in Philadelphia.

Bill Cosby (1937-) Comedian and television actor; starred in *The Cosby Show* (1984-1992); born in Philadelphia.

W. C. Fields (1880-1946) Comedian and movie actor; starred in *My Little Chickadee* and other films; born in Philadelphia.

Benjamin Franklin (1706-1790) Inventor, diplomat, and author; helped write the Declaration of Independence and the Constitution; founded a library, hospital, and fire department in Philadelphia.

Grace Kelly (1929-1982) Academy Award-winning movie actress; married Prince Rainier II of Monaco in 1956 and became Princess Grace; born in Philadelphia.

Arnold Palmer (1929-) Professional golfer; became the first to win the Masters championship four times; born in Latrobe.

Robert Peary (1856-1920) Explorer who is credited as the first person to reach the North Pole (1909); born in Cresson.

Fred Rogers (1928-) Created and starred in *Mister Rogers' Neighborhood*; born in Latrobe.

Henry Ossawa Tanner (1859-1937) Artist whose paintings had religious themes; born in Pittsburgh.

Andrew Wyeth (1917-) Artist known for his paintings of the Pennsylvania countryside; born in Chadds Ford.

Glossary

ancestor—a person from whom one is descended, such as a grandmother or a great-grandfather

colony—group of people who settle in a distant land but remain under control of their native country

descendant—a person who is born after other people in a family, such as a daughter or a grandson

immigrant—a person who comes to another country to settle

Piedmont—land at the foot of a mountain

ratify—to officially approve a law or document

reservation—land set aside for Native Americans

rural—relating to the country

surrender—to lay down arms or give up during a war

Water tumbles over a falls in Pennsylvania.

To Learn More

Clay, Rebecca. *Kidding Around Philadelphia: A Young Person's Guide to the City*. Santa Fe, N.M.: John Muir Publications, 1990.

Fradin, Dennis B. *Pennsylvania*. From Sea to Shining Sea. Chicago: Children's Press, 1994.

Kent, Deborah. *Pennsylvania*. America the Beautiful. Chicago: Children's Press, 1987.

Swain, Gwenyth. *Pennsylvania*. Hello USA. Minneapolis: Lerner Publications, 1992.

Internet Sites

City.Net Pennsylvania
http://www.city.net/countries/united_states/pennsylvania
Travel.org-Pennsylvania
http://travel.org/pennsyl.html
Commonwealth of Pennsylvania
http://www.state.pa.us/
Internet Vacation Guide-Pennsylvania
http://www.whitehawk.com/vacation/pa/

Useful Addresses

Chocolate World
Hersheypark Drive
Hershey, PA 17033

Drake Oil Well Museum
RD 3, Box 7
Titusville, PA 16354

Gettysburg National Military Park
97 Taneytown Road
Gettysburg, PA 17325

Johnstown Flood Museum
304 Washington Street
Johnstown, PA 15901

Little League Baseball Museum
Route 15 South
P.O. Box 3485
Williamsport, PA 17701

Index

Amish, 19
antislavery, 19

Battle of Gettysburg, 28

Carnegie, Andrew, 38
coal, 9, 32, 33
Constitution, 9, 27

Declaration of Independence,
   8, 25

England, 23-25, 27

farming, 14, 17, 19, 31, 33
forests, 15, 35
France, 24

Great Depression, 29
Groundhog Day, 38
Harrisburg, 37
Hershey, 9

Independence Hall, 7, 9, 35

Johnstown flood, 14

Lake Erie, 12, 14, 33
Liberty Bell, 7-9

mining, 18, 27, 29, 31, 33, 37
mushrooms, 32-33

nuclear power, 37

Penn, William, 24, 25
Philadelphia, 7, 9, 13, 17, 19,
   20, 24-25, 27, 29, 31-32,
   35-36
Pittsburgh, 9
Pocono Mountains, 13, 37
pollution, 29

slaves, 19-20
steel, 28-29, 33, 36-37, 38

Three Mile Island, 37

Underground Railroad, 20

Washington, George, 25, 27,
   36